ROSS ON WYE
Revisited

During a visit to England Woodrow Wilson, one time President of the United States, wrote "Yesterday I rode for nearly twenty miles beside the Wye, and of all the parts of England I have seen, it has most won my heart." Judging by the number of people who return to Ross on Wye and the neighbouring Wye Valley, the scenery still exerts the same effect upon visiting tourists.

ROSS ON WYE
REVISITED

by
Tim Ward

Logaston Press

LOGASTON PRESS
Little Logaston Woonton Almeley
Herefordshire HR3 6QH
logastonpress.co.uk

First published by Logaston Press 2013

ISBN 978 1 906663 71 1

Typeset by Logaston Press
and printed and bound by Bell & Bain Ltd., Glasgow

Cover: This 1905 postcard shows a view of part of the town now changed almost beyond recognition. The railway embankment running across the foreground was bulldozed in 1990 to provide soil for the gardens of the houses built on the old cattle market, whose buildings can just be seen beyond it. A man tends one of the fifty allotments in the field above the railway embankment; sadly, only a handful of these remain occupied.

Contents

The book is not divided into formal chapters or sections. Instead it starts with a short historical background to Ross, and then the text or caption accompanying each photograph leads on to that for the following illustration. We begin with the town's origins, with the church on the top of the hill and the nearby Market Place. The Wye's importance as a trade route is followed by the disruptions its floods cause, as well as the pleasure and relaxation its boating facilities provide. From trade around the Market Hall the text and photographs extend to cover the streets radiating from it. Other aspects covered include the use of Ross as a major military training camp after the creation of the Territorial Army in 1908, the demolition and replacement of the poor housing in the lower lying area of the town around the old millpond, the entertainment on offer in the cafés, pubs, cinemas, theatre and annual carnivals, a brief look at education, a review of the traffic problems after the Second World War and the arrival of the M50 Ross Spur and eastern by-pass, and an acknowledgement of the town's emergency services

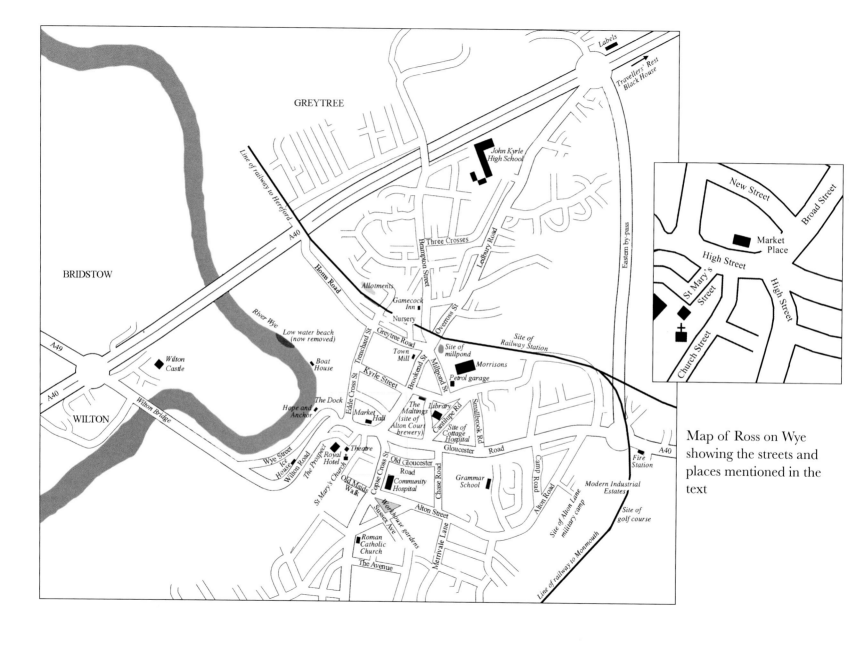

Map of Ross on Wye showing the streets and places mentioned in the text

Introduction and Acknowledgements

During the eight years that have elapsed since the publication of *The Changing Face of Ross on Wye*, I have been fortunate to acquire many more old postcards, photographs from the 1930s to 1960s and a box full of solicitors' documents. So much, in fact, that I was persuaded to embark on this second book to illustrate some more nearly forgotten aspects of life during the last two centuries of rapid change in Ross. In some cases more information has come to light, enabling me to extend and expand on information in my previous book. As ever I am indebted to the older generation of townspeople, whose memories are stirred by these old photographs. Ross people were glad to identify many photographs with names and locations, bringing to life images of otherwise anonymous scenes in the town's history. In some cases also people have freely allowed me access to their family photograph collections and memories, for which I am extremely grateful. Researching and recording some of these inevitable changes in the town where my family has now lived for two decades has been a continual pleasure, enriching my retirement years with unexpected new horizons and, in modern parlance, giving me endless job satisfaction. I apologise if I have duplicated other researchers' findings, but the interpretations are my own. Library and record office documents are available to everyone and study often throws up more questions than answers. As with research for my other books, I have unearthed more information than I could possibly include in these pages and I apologise for not including some people's stories. As much as possible I have searched for information featuring the way people of Ross on Wye lived, how circumstances changed them and the town, and the effects that some national events had locally. Needless to say, my eternal gratitude extends to my wife, Shirley, for her never-failing patiently enthusiastic and encouraging comments during her long spell of ill health. Most of the photographic material comes from my own collection. I have tried to discover the holders of the photographs' copyright where applicable, and give due acknowledgement in the relevant place.

I have used the name 'Ross' in connection with scenes before 1931, when the name was changed to Ross on Wye, which form I have used in connection with images of later date.

Much of the information that accompanies the images comes from the *Hereford Journal* 1800-1810, *The Ross Gazette* (and I must thank the paper's friendly staff), Kelly's Directories 1891-1941, Jakeman & Carver's Directory 1892, Littlebury's Directories 1867 and 1876, Frederick Cooper's account books 1895/1915, a barge owner's account book 1809/12), *The Beauties of England and Wales* by Brayley and Britton 1806, *The Gentleman's Magazine* 1817, and *The Phoenix Arises* by Robin Craig.

I also wish to thank the staff at Ross on Wye Heritage Centre, Hereford Reference Library, Hereford Record Office and Ross on Wye Library, and, though last on the list certainly not least in importance, the photographs, documents and stories from Richard Andrews, Sheila Spratley, Brian Skinner, Gordon Brown, Gordon Lucas, Roger Broomfield, Joyce Cowdery and family, Tony Bridges, George Taylor, Jim Plant, Julie Wells, Sheila Russell, Ernie Gibbens, Colin Smith, Paul Mason, Colin Fears, Roger Burton, Mary Sinclair Powell and Kevin Minton, all of which I found invaluable. My sincere apologies to anyone I have inadvertently not mentioned above.

Ross on Wye

The lack of archaeological evidence does not mean that the fertile land around Ross on Wye has not been inhabited for millennia. Indeed, the nearby hillfort of Chase Hill Camp, covering 19 acres, shows that from the Bronze Age (*c*. BC 1000) to the time of the Roman invasion in AD 43 a large and well organised population could defend itself in times of stress. Their Celtic word 'rhos' for a hill or promontory gave the town its name, Ross.

The recent discovery of a Roman look-out post at the Prospect, high above the Wye, shows a hitherto unknown Roman military presence. It was probably part of the security system for the ford and river crossing at Wilton and the road through to Ariconium, the valuable iron-working area four miles to the east near Weston under Penyard. Evidence has not yet emerged to show that the place that became Ross remained inhabited after the Roman withdrawal in AD 410. What is certain is that sometime during the subsequent six centuries and long before its record in 1086 in the Domesday Book, it had become an Anglo-Saxon settlement, built on the Bishop of Hereford's extensive lands. Part of the town is believed to have developed along the High Street round the church on the hill, and part on the lower land in Brookend Street near the Town Mill, which, though rebuilt several times, remained in use for a thousand years.

During Stephen's troubled reign (1135-54) he granted the Bishop of Hereford the right to hold a market at Ross. In reality this gave the bishop an extra income from a legalised toll on the traders, who had almost certainly held an unregulated market there for centuries.

The triangular market place developed beside the road junction to Hereford, Ledbury and the Forest of Dean. Shops, houses and inns soon bordered it, built on burgage plots laid out on the bishop's land. These plots stretched on both sides of the streets from Town Mill to High Street, forming the basis of the present town, unchanged by the passing centuries.

From the bishop's extensive estate recorded in Domesday Book, we can assume the presence of a church close to the site of the present building. The present church was begun in 1280, and itself has undergone many alterations and enlargements.

When the adjacent Royal Hotel was being built in 1837, the discovery of cellars and a prison revealed it had been built on the site of the Bishop's Palace, abandoned in the 14th century after the ravages of the Black Death. Despite set backs from outbreaks of plague, food shortages and border skirmishes, by the 17th century Ross had grown from a self-sufficient market town to a small manufacturing town. Its commercial links were mainly along the river Wye, as roads were unsurfaced tracks, impassable for much of the year to wheeled traffic. As expected from a market town in a fertile farming area, agricultural produce in the form of corn, cheese, leather, bark, timber, horses and farm animals, woven baskets of all sizes, rope, cider and woollen products all contributed at different periods to the town's prosperity, as revealed by some fine timbered buildings. From the 16th century workshops making gloves, hats, shoes and nails were established, as well as tanneries and at least two fulling mills supporting the woollen industry.

Until the Civil War national politics had affected Ross very little. Indeed, the town had given up its right to send Members to Parliament in 1360 because of the cost of two shillings a day each! Although Ross saw no battles in the Civil War, the disruption and plunder inflicted on the town and countryside by the manoeuvres of the conflicting armies was immense. Nearby Goodrich Castle

Wilton Castle

was occupied first in 1642 by the Parliamentarians based in Gloucester and then by a Royalist garrison from 1644-46. The unpaid Scots army besieging Hereford for Parliament inflicted the worst depredations on the area, plundering goods worth thousands of pounds in the county including £1,189 worth from Ross. It was during this period that one arch of Wilton Bridge was demolished and Sir John Bridges, who by endeavouring to remain neutral in the conflict had upset the Royalists, found his home at Wilton Castle burned down on returning from a church service. Religious conflict replaced open warfare after the fighting was over, as the Puritans tried to install their ministers to assert their pious beliefs.

Stability returned with King Charles II. Later, as wealth accumulated in the 18th and 19th centuries, a middle class of lawyers, bankers, shopkeepers and merchants emerged and built substantial houses on the edge of town, away from the workers' poor dwellings near their workplaces in the town centre.

Industries continued to grow as more people, some displaced by land enclosures, moved into the town's small crowded houses, providing a workforce for local industries. Beer was brewed on a small scale at most public houses until Alton Court Brewery Company's massive brewery was built in 1856. The fine wool from the local Ryeland sheep was the basis for a trade in woollen products from at least two fulling mills. Thousands of gallons of cider were sent by barge to Bristol and Chepstow each year. Leather was produced in large quantities from smelly tanneries utilising abundant nearby supplies of cheap oak bark. Some of this leather was used for making the boots and shoes for which Ross became well known, and some to meet the insatiable demand for harnesses for the thousands of horses and oxen powering agriculture and transport. New Street became a centre for the nail-making industry which developed from the mid 1600s to the mid 1800s, when iron foundries replaced them, making agricultural implements. When the Royal Hotel controversially took over part of the site in 1837, the long established animal market for horses, sheep, pigs and cattle at the Pounds was moved to Swan Corner at the top of Edde Cross Street and New Street. For thirty years the resultant squalor and filth was tolerated until the Town Commissioners were forced to open a purpose-built cattle market in September 1871 between the railway embankment and Homs Road. After 1988, when a new cattle market was built outside the town beside the by-pass, a housing development, Old Market Close, soon covered the old site. Ross's growth continues as I write (in January 2013) with more flats being built there. Corn continued to be ground into flour in Town Mill until 1895 when steam replaced water power. The full effects of the Industrial Revolution arrived with the Hereford, Ross and Gloucester railway in 1855. Connected by a rapid communication system to the rest of the country, it brought to an end the stagecoach era and most of the Wye's barge traffic.

Opposite: Most apparent in this 1932 aerial view of Ross on Wye from the south-east is the lack of houses in the Sussex Gardens area in the foreground. The fourth building on the left on Walford Road (and near the road junction towards the centre of the photograph) is the then recently built Roman Catholic Church, before its screen of trees grew. The Bishop of Llandaff laid its foundation stone on 10 September 1930 and when services commenced six months later the congregation were able to move from their temporary room in the Crofts. For over a hundred years the triangular part of Dean Hill Park nearest the workhouse in the centre of the photograph was cultivated by able-bodied inmates as a vegetable garden to grow crops needed for the staff and residents' meals. Neat rows of vegetables can clearly be seen in the triangle of land now given over to a popular children's play area. Any surplus produce was sold to help finance the institution. People with learning difficulties used the huge old building after its closure as a workhouse until it was finally demolished and replaced by the new Community Hospital.

Left: An aerial view of St Mary's church and the adjacent areas of Ross in about 1930. The oldest part of the present church dates from 1328. Since then wealthy benefactors have built further aisles, refurbished the interior and added a tower and steeple with a peal of eight bells. In the central foreground, standing in its spacious gardens, is the old rectory, demolished in 1936 as uneconomic to maintain. A smaller replacement was built in a corner of the gardens. To the left of the church, screened by trees, is the Prospect, famous for its glorious views over the horseshoe bend in the river Wye to distant hills beyond. Note there are no trees on the further bank of the Wye, a reminder that from 1811-56 they were cleared to allow horses to haul barges full of coal to Hereford.

St Mary's church has been rebuilt and altered many times during its lifetime. A major refurbishment was completed in 1862 when over £2,000 was spent on the interior. Note on the right in the trees' shadow a First World War German artillery gun, later melted down in the Second World War during a shortage of suitable metal for armaments.

In their 1805 book *The Beauties of England and Wales*, Brayley and Britton wrote 'The Prospect Ground, as it is called, adjoining the Church-yard, and the Walk that extends thence for nearly a mile to the southward, were formed by his [John Kyrle's] liberality; but they are not preserved in that order which his memory demands. The Prospect Ground is now merely a field, yet enough remains to show that he intended it for a parterre; and the Walk has been deprived of many of the trees that formerly shaded it, together with the seats for the weary traveller's repose; the Summer house, also, at the termination of the walk, is now in a state of decay. Along the edges of the rock which forms the foundation of this natural terrace, the Sand Martin digs his hollow nest.'

John Kyrle was born in Dymock in 1637, the son of a wealthy family, who were able to complete his education by sending him to Oxford University. He inherited his father's home opposite the Market Hall in 1650, at the end of the Civil War troubles, a conflict which could have sparked his benevolence to his fellow townspeople. In addition to helping young married couples, he gave much of the income from his estate of £500 per year to the needy, installed a water supply from the river to the town, and helped to rebuild the church steeple. Towards the end of his life he planned and laid out gardens on the Prospect, where his intentions were thwarted by events after his death in 1724. Somewhat naively Kyrle had leased the Prospect in 1699 to William Fisher, farmer and landlord of the nearby Pounds Inn 'subject to a right of the inhabitants of Ross to walk therein' for five hundred years.

Despite this clause Fisher kept his pigs there, ruining John Kyrle's carefully constructed walks and gardens. Vandals added to the destruction by wrecking a fountain and a sundial Kyrle had provided for everyone's enjoyment. In 1810 Kyrle's descendants sold his properties in Ross, including his house, then the King's Arms, which was advertised as suitable for easily dividing into two shops. Also included was the lease of the Prospect, which the current lessee, Elizabeth Thomas, had sublet to Mr Tristram for an annual rent of £5. Though the Prospect was not of any great size, it was one of the first public town parks in the land and was still in good enough condition to host a party for a thousand people to celebrate the passing of the great Reform Act of 1832, which ultimately led to everyone's right to vote. After 1837, however, John Barrett, who previously owned the Swan Hotel, bought the lease, built the Royal Hotel, and enclosed the whole Prospect for pleasure gardens for his hotel clients' exclusive use. In a period of our history when the seldom contested enclosure of common land was taking place in every county, Barrett probably considered his purchase of the lease of the Prospect and the exclusion of the townspeople would go unnoticed and unopposed. His big mistake was to underestimate the townspeople, for they realised they were in grave danger of losing the Prospect completely and permanently, and for the next thirty years they fought to regain what they regarded as the legalised theft of their open space.

On 3 December 1839 the sober middle class citizens of Ross formed a committee and started a subscription list to raise money to fight Barrett's high-handed actions through the courts. Others wanted to take more direct action, but after the disturbances over certain land enclosures, the Swing riots, the upheavals over Parliamentary reform, the Chartists' agitation and the beginnings of trade unionism, authority hated any form of public disorder so much that ordinary people involved in riotous meetings could face a long prison sentence or transportation for quite minor breaches of the peace. In 1848, with little progress on the issue having been made and in what became known as a year of revolution throughout Europe, a riot finally broke out in July as Ross citizens tried unsuccessfully to regain their right to access the Prospect. Defeated but not beaten, the issue did not go away as townsfolk returned again to try to assert what they saw as their rights the following year. Their resentment simmered on until 1863, when another attempt at protest failed.

Matters came to a head one Saturday night in 1869 when refusal to allow the band of the Ross Rifle Volunteer Corps to perform in the Prospect led to skirmishes. The following Monday, 12 July, the most serious riot broke out. A group of 'youths and artisans', egged on by a crowd of hundreds, destroyed the Royal Hotel's gardens and burnt hedges and fences, broke into the billiard room, vandalised a cloakroom and broke windows. Wooden fences and other flammable items soon became part of a huge bonfire that illuminated the nearby church tower. In celebratory mood and led by the music of a band, members of the Barrel (Inn) Friendly Society celebrated their anniversary by parading round the destroyed gardens to re-establish everyone's right to do so. In tune with the mood of the town, the local constabulary did not intervene, regarding the disputed access as a civil matter and tacitly acknowledging the people's right to walk there. The following day a posse of policemen armed with cutlasses were hurriedly sent from Hereford to preserve the Queen's peace, but were soon withdrawn. Embarrassed by events, the Town Commissioners belatedly and ineffectually tried to intervene. Protests finally died down in 1870 when Thomas Blake, another resident benefactor of the town in the style of John Kyrle, was able to make use of his position as secretary of the Ross Royal Hotel Company Ltd to anonymously buy the Royal Hotel with its disputed grounds from Thomas Roper and install a manageress to run it. Unaware of Blake's intended benevolence, intruders created one last serious disturbance on 4 August 1870, destroying the Royal's vegetable garden and toppling a wall which was being built to give hotel guests more privacy. Two years later, in his own quiet way and without any public announcement, Blake was able to transfer the tract of land now known as the Prospect to the town in perpetuity.

On 29 February 1872 the *Ross Gazette* reported that 'the improvement already effected in laying out this handsome spot of ground is so great that it promises, when finished, to be a place that our absent friends and townsmen will hardly recognise when they return to Ross. The sward has been taken up to allow of the hollow places to be filled in and the elevated parts have been sliced off so as to make it level as a billiard board. A broad pathway with neat sloping bank on the South East side has been cut out and another through the centre leading to the old ivy covered gateway which will be thrown open in the event of the Bishop's permission being given. A large staff of men have been employed for the last three weeks and are doing their work exceedingly well. In a week or two more the Prospect will be converted into a delightful walking way.' And so it remains.

A print showing John Kyrle's original summer house, where he spent many hours overlooking his garden and bowling green. What is now known as John Kyrle's summer house was built in 1834 when this building had become dilapidated. A careful search in the private car park off Church Street reveals the overgrown ruins of the brick arch beneath the doorway – all that is left of John Kyrle's elegant little building. The roofscape in the background has hardly changed in the two hundred years since a Mr or Ms Watkins drew the scene. It seems such a shame that, when so much is made of John Kyrle's name in Ross on Wye, the 300-year-old remains of his summer house should just be allowed to disintegrate into a heap of anonymous rubble.

Wide lawns surround the old rectory in Edwardian days when the Rev. Edward Winnington-Ingram was rector. In 1936, finding the old rectory too costly to maintain, the church built a new one in a corner of the garden. For a time the police station and other offices occupied the old building, and after its demolition a doctor's surgery, a much needed police station and the new houses in St Mary's Close were built in the former gardens convenient to the town centre. Now only parts of the garden wall bordering Old Maid's Walk remain.

This 1860 photograph is an enlargement of a 100mm x 60mm early photograph called, due to its size, a *carte-de-visite* as such photographs were the same size as visiting cards much used by wealthy Victorians when socialising. Millions of these little cards, usually portraits of people, were produced until they went out of fashion about 1900. Views in this small format are rare, and this photograph of St Mary's church and churchyard is the earliest in my collection.

Prominent in the foreground is a graceful monument designed by Sir Gilbert Scott, famous for creating the Albert Memorial and St Pancras Station. The churchyard was extended in 1858 and according to Littlebury's 1876 *Directory* one of the first monuments placed on the new ground was this slender cross in the early English style to the memory of Mabel Fiennes, daughter of George Strong (of the Chase in Gloucester Road). Three years later the 14-year-old was joined by her 18-year-old sister Gertrude Pollexfen. We can only wonder if the small group examining the elegant and expensive memorial were members of the Strong family. The surrounding railings were probably removed in the drive for scrap iron in the Second World War. After about a hundred years, for safety reasons the tall shaft was removed, completely spoiling the memorial's appearance.

After its beauty was 'discovered' in 1765 tourists flocked to Ross to enjoy the scenery of the Wye valley after reading of its attractions, extolled in numerous directories and guide books. This 1840s engraving of the river Wye at Ross reminds us that for centuries before the arrival of the railway, the river was of vital importance to the economic life of the towns and villages on its banks as well as much of the surrounding countryside.

A number of different types of rivercraft are depicted. On the left, two men haul a pleasure boat towards its base at the Hope and Anchor. Tourists were protected from the elements in its canopied cabin, where a central table contained lockers for food, drinks and possessions. Parties of up to twenty people travelled in comfort and style on the cushioned seats. On the right a rowing boat takes three tourists for a short trip; behind them a fisherman paddles his coracle, a relic of thousands of years' use on the Wye, which finally disappeared at the end of the 19th century. On 15 August 1871 the *Ross Gazette* reported a regatta at the Hope and Anchor where a coracle race attracted five entries. T. Morgan and C. Morgan of Monmouth came in first and second, with S. Jones of Ross third. To the left of the coracle, the crew of a barge from Hereford make use of a favourable wind on its square sail as well as the craft's oars to propel the vessel downstream. Two horses on the towing path on the west bank haul a laden barge towards Hereford. To avoid snagging the bushes that grew on the river's bank, the tow rope was attached half way up the mast. By attaching it to the mast and *not* the bow, the tendency to pull the barge towards the bank was lessened, making the steersman's job easier.

Despite some landowners' opposition, a towing path was opened in 1811, criss-crossing the river at various points (where ferries were provided to carry the horses over) to avoid land owned by opponents to the scheme. Unemployment was high at the time, so the teams of men bow-haulers bitterly resented the arrival of the towing path, fearing horses would deprive them of work. Barges, varying in capacity from 12 to 70 tons, were built on the banks of the Wye as far upstream as Hay on Wye. They were crewed by up to five men, to row, quant or set the sails to favourable winds to carry loads of building materials, Welsh slates, road-stone, coal, lime, seeds, corn, wine, spirits, furniture and manu-factured goods up-river to Monmouth, Ross, Hereford and beyond. Corn, hops, cider and timber, the products of Herefordshire's rich farmland, were shipped downstream to Chepstow and Bristol for delivery to distant parts of the country. Their flat-bottomed build allowed barges to load or unload cargoes at the numerous wharves along the river or directly onto convenient river banks.

Built on the top of the hill or 'rhos' (the Welsh word from which the town takes its name) in 1837, the Royal Hotel, seen to the right of St Mary's church tower and the battlemented circular gazebo, has overlooked Ross's tranquil waterside and witnessed many changes. In this 1932 photograph cattle graze the lush summer grass in the Rope Walk meadow. In 1960, during the construction of the A40, this 4-acre meadow was transformed by Tarmac Civil Engineering, who needed somewhere to dispose of the surplus subsoil from the road cutting at nearby Greytree. Four thousand tons of subsoil was spread on the Rope Walk Meadow and the topsoil replaced, at no cost to the council. Thanking Tarmac, the chairman of Ross Urban District Council, W.S. Little, called this 'the greatest improvement to the river area in 100 years'. The pasture has now become an asset to the town, boasting a children's play area, a riverside path and seats for people to relax, picnic and play on the trimmed grass. For years this was the pleasant venue for the Ross on Wye Music Festival. The sheds at the dock beside the Hope and Anchor originally housed barge freight. When this finished, they were used for storage and workshops, and until the 1930s they housed William Dowell's basket-making business.

Richard (Dickie) Edwin Davies, a prolific Ross photographer, published this postcard in the 1930s. On the left it shows the wooden hull of the *Wilton Castle* pleasure steamer lying half submerged beside the dock. In 1902 Henry Dowell launched this 65-foot long stern-wheeled paddle steamer, built to his own design from his life-long knowledge of the Wye. The boat's initial enthusiastic holiday trade disappeared as people found other holiday interests. The novelty over and with profits dwindling, Henry Dowell tried unsuccessfully to sell it in 1912. The following year he stripped it of everything usable or saleable and abandoned the hull on the river bank. At a later date it was surrounded by timber scaffolding as both protection and warning to river users of its position. A group of people stand on the wooden landing stage where a ferry operated on regatta days to carry spectators across the river to watch events from Oak Meadow. The gazebo on the skyline in the centre of the photograph was a folly erected in the 1830s when Wilton Road was cut across the cliff face to create a gentler approach road to Ross for the increasing numbers of stagecoaches and other horse-drawn traffic arriving from Wales and Hereford. The walls on Swan Corner, the British and Foreign School and the town gaol in New Street were built in the same mock medieval style from the sandstone excavated to build Wilton Road.

Built by James Barrett for over £15,000 in 1837, the Royal Hotel still dominates the Ross on Wye skyline. In 1867 George Cornelius Baynham was listed as a jobmaster – a livery stable keeper who jobbed (hired) out horses and carriages. With his son Walter, he operated a variety of horse-drawn carriages and charabancs from the Royal Hotel to the Forest of Dean, Monmouth and Chepstow. Following in the family business, Walter's daughter, Irene, became owner of a successful and well-remembered car hire and coach firm based first at the Royal. This 1937 photograph shows one of her buses awaiting passengers. Note the BP petrol pumps sited on the edge of the pavement for the convenience of cars. The gazebo tower is visible on the far right.

Over fifty local people, mostly mothers and children, enjoy a cooling paddle or swim in the Wye. This pebble bank was uncovered during one of the hot, dry summers during the 1930s, which lowered the water level drastically. People's attitudes to river bathing, however, were soon to change due to the danger to health from polluted river water. As there was no swimming pool in Ross on Wye, parents raised £2,000 to build a swimming pool at the Grammar School in 1960, so that their children could learn to swim in safety. The public swimming pool was not built until 1973. This convenient 'beach' was just upstream from the Rowing Club boat house. Early in the 1990s the Rowing Club employed a bulldozer and scraper to dredge this natural beach out of existence to deepen and widen the river's course for their increasingly popular and well attended regattas.

The Wye is prone to flooding, and this view is of a major flood on 28 August 1912. In the foreground is the derelict ice house built by Samuel Llewellyn and surrounded by colourful advertising hoardings. Llewellyn ran a number of business ventures, including selling coal at the railway station yard and running a fruit, game and fish shop in High Street. In the autumn of 1870 he engaged Mr Ward, of Beaumont Villa, Ashfield, to construct a specially designed four-storey ice house measuring 33 feet high by 26 feet long and 21 feet wide, (reportedly) the largest in the west of England. He positioned it against the north-facing cliff, where its four feet thick walls protected its precious store of ice from thawing in the

warmth of the summer sun. The walls were further insulated with sawdust to protect the five hundred tons of ice from melting. In the extremely cold winter of 1870/71, seven men collected clean ice from Alton Court springs on the edge of the town, rather than from the much nearer – but dirtier – river Wye. Llewellyn's investment was repaid the following summer, when although he lost a few inches of ice to melting he was able to use the rest in his High Street fruit, game and fishmonger's shop in the place of expensive imported ice from Norway. In the days when domestic refrigerators were unknown he was able to supply ice to anyone needing it for cool drinks or food storage, but despite the ice house's initial success, it fell out of use as commercial refrigeration improved. By 1912 Frederick Cooper, a local auctioneer, had surrounded the building with advertising hoardings. His advertising rates varied between the ten shillings a year he charged Passey and Hall, a local garage and the guinea, (£1-1s) he charged Allen Bros., owners of a fleet of Transatlantic passenger liners sailing from Liverpool with emigrants hoping for a better life abroad.

Lying below the level of the Rudhall Brook, Brookend Street has always been vulnerable to floods. The earliest flood report in the *Ross Gazette* on 14 November 1875 stated 'The Rudhall Brook overflowed through Queen Street [the original name of Station Street] into Alton Court Brewery Company's yard causing huge damage and floating empty beer barrels away. Brookend Street flooded to a depth of three to four feet doing a colossal amount of damage.'

In March 1947, following a winter of heavy snowfalls, many low-lying parts of the country were affected by widespread flooding. As the snow melted, Ross on Wye suffered similarly. A boy checks the depth of the floodwater in Brookend Street on 20 March to see if his wellies are tall enough to let him wade any further without getting wet feet. Floodwater severely damaged Connie Dean's shop on the left and affected all the others in the street. Despite official promises to take action to prevent such floods, they still recurred with regular and depressing monotony for the next sixty years.

Two lads, full of the bravado of youth, wade along the centre of the flooded Brookend Street in 1970. On the left they pass Danter's Magnet Snack Bar and Ace Arcade, which were popular venues for teenagers in the 1960s and 1970s. These have since been incorporated into the Barrel Inn, whose entrance was then at the side of the building. In the mid 19th century the Barrel Inn was a much larger establishment, housing its own small brewery and supplying pubs as far away as Fownhope. In Edwardian times its proprietor, Charles Mew, donated barrels of beer to the Ross Union Workhouse for the inmates' Christmas meals. In 1920 the Barrel was swallowed up by the Alton Court Brewery Company. A flood of this depth was not quite high enough to enter the shops, though the disruption it caused to trade and traffic was considerable. As a health precaution, when the flood water had subsided and before the road was re-opened to traffic, Ross on Wye's Fire Brigade had the unpleasant task of hosing the filthy, smelly residue into the drains from which much of it had originated.

Photographed in June 1910 from Springfield House in Brampton Road this spectacular show of lightning displays the power of a fierce electrical storm. Whilst storms can cause some local flooding, the Wye floods due to the sheer amount of run off it is taking from Wales, and therefore close attention is paid to rainfall levels in central Wales. Ross on Wye in fact has one of the oldest weather observatories in the country, started by Henry Southall in 1859. Frederick J. Parsons took over his self-appointed task as observer in 1914 and from the 1920s daily reported local weather conditions to the Meteorological Office. This data helped prepare national weather forecasts. Acknowledging its importance, Ian McCaskill opened the present Ross on Wye Weather Station on 16 May 1985. For many years the *Ross Gazette* has published Ross on Wye's detailed monthly weather records.

For centuries, much of the commercial life of the town has been centred round the stone-arched Market Hall in the centre of the picture. Second to St Mary's as the town's chief landmark, it was built in the mid 17th century of local Old Red Sandstone close to the site of the original Booth Hall. In this picture of 1810, Underhill, the building to the left of the Market Hall, occupied much of what had been the market place, the result of a gradual encroachment outside the original burgage plots. This had slowly diminished the size of the market place since its charter granted in 1138. By 1862 the building had fallen into such a state of decay that the Town Commissioners demolished it, recreating the extent of the original Market Place and the view of the Market Hall we now know.

An unusually quiet view up High Street from the Market Hall and (beyond the Old Gloucester Road junction) Copse Cross Street, with no traffic in view. Externally few apparent changes to the buildings have taken place since this 1950s photograph. Dating from the 15th century, the Rosswyn Hotel (on the left) was rebuilt over the years and contained a number of historic features including an Elizabethan fireplace, a Jacobean staircase, 17th-century carvings and a probable priest hole in the cellar. Named Chepstow House, during the first half of the 20th century it was home to a succession of doctors until the Second World War, when it was requisitioned by the Army. After the soldiers left in 1945, the government paid a large sum in compensation for damage they had caused including when, during a fuel shortage, they had burnt the stairs to keep warm. Mr Skinner opened the Rosswyn first as a B&B which soon developed into a comfortable hotel. Regulars enjoyed many a quiet drink there and it is fondly remembered as a venue for numerous parties and celebrations until a disastrous fire on 10 November 2004 forced its hurried evacuation and final closure.

An idyllic view looking up Broad Street in 1910 in bright summer sunshine, the Market Hall standing about a hundred yards further along the road. The shopkeepers had to extend their sunshades to protect their wares from both the sunshine and the dust blowing from streets that were not surfaced until 1912. Note the cast iron bollards on the corners of Station Street on the immediate left to prevent vehicles mounting the pavements as they turned the corner. In 1939 the Roxy cinema replaced the white shop building on the left. This in turn was demolished in the 1970s to be replaced by the Maltings Arcade of modern shops.

A winter view in 1908 looking down Broad Street from the Market Place in front of the Market Hall, photographed by R.E. Davies. On the left were William Watkins' grocery shop and Kiddle's tailors and outfitters. The pony and trap stand outside the Crown and Sceptre. The shops on the right included W.H. Smith (booksellers), G. Eltome (clothiers and hosiers) and Innell & Wharton (ironmongers). In those quiet days a hundred years ago a dog could safely sleep in the middle of the street!

In 1908, a lady intent on posting her letter hurries past a scene of confusion outside the National Provincial bank, with the Market Hall in the background. While interested spectators crowded round, workmen and onlookers try to repair an overturned farm wagon before clearing its tumbled load of wheat sheaves blocking the bank's doorway. A terse paragraph, rather like a police report, appeared in the *Ross Gazette* on 30 July describing the event. 'Waggon Load of Straw Overturns. Whilst proceeding along High Street on Tuesday morning [28 July 1908], and when approaching the National Provincial bank, on the corner of Gloucester Road, a large waggon load of straw suddenly overturned, falling with force against the front entrance of the bank. At the time this happened an old gentleman named Robbins was passing and he, unfortunately, was knocked down by the falling straw, but luckily escaped with only a shaking. The cause of the upset is attributed to the pin coming out from underneath the waggon, which belonged to Mrs Miles, Netherton, Pencoyd.'

In the early 1930s a motorcycle drives slowly along an otherwise almost traffic-free High Street past Heal's the drapers, with the Market Hall in the background. On the left a sign for the New Theatre Cinema hangs prominently over the Corn Exchange door. In the 1920s Garfield Prickett leased the building and from 1929 ran a cinema in the 750 capacity hall in competition with Edwin Dekins' Kyrle Picture Palace. From its opening in 1862 the hall was used for its primary function as a corn exchange. Later it hosted a variety of events in the town's social life including lectures, concerts, public meetings, boxing matches, a commercial school (in 1922) and even roller skating competitions, until it was destroyed by fire in February 1938. The upper floor has been refurbished as Ross on Wye's Council Chamber.

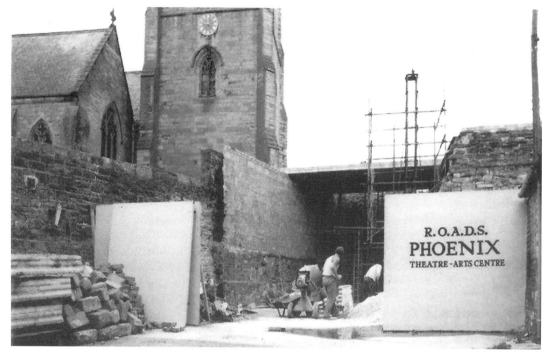

A short way up St Mary's Street, off to the right of the previous photograph, is the current Ross theatre. Ross Operatic and Drama Society (ROADS) had for years staged popular productions in different locations in the town, but needed premises of its own. Seizing an opportunity in 1971, it bought the old fire station building for £2,000 and began the long task of converting it into a purpose-built theatre. In 1973, to keep costs to the minimum, keen members undertook much of the construction work themselves. In the days before National Lottery funds were available for such an enterprise, the society had to raise all the necessary finance itself. No one could foresee that, because of planning delays as well as difficulties in raising the amount of money needed, work would continue for the next ten years. After much hard work, on 15 October 1983, the Lord Lieutenant, Captain Thomas Dunne, opened their new theatre, the Phoenix. Nineteen years later it was extended into the building we know today.

The Tudor Tea Rooms at 38 High Street, on the other side of the road from the Market Hall, was just one of many cafés in Ross competing for whatever trade was available from both tourists and locals. For many years prior to his death, James Barnwell, a grocer in the nearby Market Place, owned the property. After his death in the late 1920s the property passed through the hands of a number of different owners and tenants during the difficult years of the Depression. Winston Vaughan was the proprietor at the time of this 1930s photograph, paying £480 per year rent and charging his customers 2s 6d (12½p) for luncheon. Even in 1941, during a period of severe rationing during the Second World War, the Tudor Tea Rooms could still offer Table D'Hôte and À la Carte Luncheons, Afternoon Teas & Morning Coffee and Snacks.

Like many other small shops in Ross, the Pottery Pantry in the High Street was home to a variety of businesses and owners. In the late 1950s and early 1960s 'Potters' was variously a tea room and a pottery shop run by Peter Plunkett-Morris, a sweet shop run by Mr and Mrs Turpin and then by Mr and Mrs Trow. Later Mr Frost sold milk and dairy products there. Owners used the rooms behind the small front shop as a café. The premises changed hands several more times in the following decades, later becoming Cloisters restaurant. A generation of Ross teenagers, too young and penniless to visit pubs, hung out in the café, especially at weekends and in the evenings, where coffee was cheap and a juke box continually played the music of the sixties. In this relaxed atmosphere teenage romances flourished, leading in several cases to marriages. Some prim parents tended to regard 'Potters' as a den of iniquity and banned their children from going there. However, Mr and Mrs Trow's young customers fondly remember them as very tolerant and understanding, allowing their penniless clientele to stay all evening for the price of one coffee!

From 1860 to 1911 Richard Powle ran his family's printing and stationery business at 35 High Street in this old timbered building, which at one time had been John Kyrle's home. Powle found it made good business sense to use the famous man's name and the building's history whenever possible and erected a large sign emblazoned 'HOUSE OF JOHN KYRLE' over the entrance to attract visitors. H.C. Jefferies continued to use the link with John Kyrle as a publicity ploy after he bought the long-established business in 1911, although he also described it as 'formerly Powles' in recognition of his predecessor's long association with the business. Racks of Jefferies' postcards hang in the doorway. With different owners this shop has remained a stationer's shop for over one hundred and fifty years, now trading as Colmans.

This 1890s photograph shows tiny front gardens in front of the houses bordering Gloucester Road, the spaces long since incorporated into the buildings and transformed into a variety of shop premises. Until 1910-12 Ross's roads were not surfaced, so hazards to pedestrians in Victoria's reign included dust in summer and mud when it rained. Maybe worse were the never-ending heaps of horse droppings left by the hundreds of horses used for transporting goods and people around the town. Pollution from cars, which now tend to clog this busy street, might be hazardous to our health but at least the streets are clean. Gloucester Road did not exist until the 1820s when the Town Commissioners feared the town would lose its valuable coach trade unless the road from Gloucester was improved. Some premises built on the mediaeval burgage plots between the present Natwest Bank and the now demolished George Hotel were bought and pulled down, creating the Cross we know today. This new road bypassed the narrow Old Gloucester Road, where sixteen stage-coaches were reported to pass daily. Their tired horses were changed at the town's inns and hotels for fresh animals. The George Hotel, for example, had stabling for a hundred horses.

Taken from further out of town along the Gloucester Road than the photograph opposite, this photograph dates to the time of the Second World War. The evidence for this lies in the black and white painted kerb stones on the corner of Chase Road and the striped lamp posts. In the wartime blackout, street lights were turned off and car headlights dimmed to make attack by enemy aircraft at night more difficult. Kerb stones and lamp posts were painted black and white to make them more visible and improve safety for pedestrians. Despite these precautions, the number of previously avoidable accidents rose considerably. Partly because of wartime restrictions and petrol rationing, few cars are to be seen.

In the centuries before the advent of the internal combustion engine, when horses and oxen powered all road transport and heavy farm work, blacksmiths could be found in every town and village. Shoeing children's riding ponies or massive shire horses, repairing broken parts of farm machinery, coaches or wagons was all part of a smith's daily work. In the early 1900s Joseph (Joe) Seymour lived comfortably in Bridstow and owned this prime site at 8 Gloucester Road. He worked with his men and stands on the left of the group beside a smartly dressed groom holding two hunters. For a time Colin Smith's greengrocery shop occupied the site until a modern shop was built in 2004/5.

For a brief interlude between the pre-eminence of the horse and that of the internal combustion engine, there was a period where horses shared the road with the steam engine. In this picture, a traction engine pauses outside the Council School in Cantilupe Road on its way to Kemps' sawmill with the trunk of a massive oak tree.

Left: In the first decades of the 20th century Llewellyn and Son operated a large fleet of mostly Sentinel steam lorries for their coal and haulage business in Station Street, convenient to the railway station goods yard. Their solid construction and moderate speed made them ideal vehicles for local deliveries on poor roads. To minimise damage to the weak road surfaces of the day, owners of heavy steam engines were encouraged to use rubber tyres to cover their steel wheels. Llewellyn proudly used this photograph of this gleaming 16-ton showman's engine recently fitted with new rubber tyres in their workshops as an example of his work.

Opposite: Henry Ford was the first man to mass produce a motor car, the Model T Ford. From October 1917 at Dearborn in the USA, he also commenced making the world's first mass production tractor, the Model F Fordson. Exports to Britain started immediately, but too late to have any impact on wartime food production. Early in 1918, eleven of the 7,000 Fordson tractors earmarked for the UK were delivered for work on farms in the Ross area. Watched by a group of convalescent soldiers and a few townspeople, they were exhibited in the Market Place before setting to work. The drivers included two Women's Land Army girls, four civilians and five soldiers. These soldiers were recuperating from wounds in a convalescent hospital in Gloucester Road and wore distinctive hospital blue invalid uniforms. According to advertisements in the *Ross Gazette*, Model F Fordson tractors cost £250 plus £40 for an Oliver plough, 'deliveries from the USA permitting'. Lower priced than their competitors, as more became available after the war, they soon became the farmers' tractor of choice. Note the thin metal tyres on the rear wheels, necessary to prevent the wheel cleats damaging the weak road surfaces of the time. Drivers had to remove these tyres before field work could begin.

37

For the Herefordshire Volunteer Infantry at the turn of the century, motorised transport had not yet arrived. In those days, before radio, rapid communication was a problem for Army units. Semaphore was one answer. Another solution was to relay messages to and from headquarters by bicycle; cycling was also an efficient method of moving troops rapidly from place to place, preferred by many to marching. This is a bicycle detachment of Ross's B Company, lined up in Cantilupe Road for a souvenir photograph *circa* 1900. The soldiers of B Company also earned themselves a reputation as marksmen by winning many rifle-shooting competitions, profiting from regular practice on the local range at Alton Court. In 1908, with the possibility of a European war approaching, Haldane, the Army Minister, instituted a series of reforms under which the Volunteers were disbanded and replaced by a reorganised and more efficient Territorial Army.

Not long after Haldane's reforms, Territorial soldiers of the Northamptonshire Regiment parade in Alton Lane (now Alton Road) camp during their fortnight's training in August 1912. As part of the reforms, Ross was designated one of eleven approved camps in the country for training territorial soldiers. In the summer months battalions of the Territorial Army visited the camp in Alton Lane for a fortnight or three weeks' training under canvas beside Ross's nine hole golf course. Their stay was reckoned to inject about £5,000 per week into the economy of the Ross area, which was much appreciated by local businesses. The same units often returned year after year. Six or eight men and their equipment were housed in each canvas bell tent. Permanent buildings housed the camp administration and the soldiers' cookhouse. For the duration of the camp, Ross Golf Club members leased half their club house for use as the Officers' Mess. The houses in the background are in Camp Road.

At the end of a route march a battalion of the Staffordshire Regiment heads back to camp along Gloucester Road, watched by groups of admiring young men and girls. Development along the south side of the street was not then complete and hoardings advertising Dekins' antique furniture screen a waste site beside the offices of William Woolf's haulage and removal firm.

Sunday church parades during the Territorials' stay at Ross were obligatory, though Roman Catholics and Nonconformists could attend their own services. The band of the Staffordshire Regiment leads the battalion into camp on their return from church past a notice proclaiming Ross Golf Links. It is evident from reports in the *Ross Gazette* and the *Hereford Journal* that Ross had long been accustomed to a military presence as soldiers in transit between barracks, on manoeuvres or en route to training areas and artillery ranges in Wales stopped at Ross overnight, though not necessarily at the campsite in Alton Road. Two hundred years ago soldiers in transit marched to their new posting and were billeted in pubs and inns at a fixed charge per night.

Traditionally the King's Shropshire Light Infantry recruited many men from Herefordshire into their ranks. In 1913 the KSLI made use of the training facilities at Ross; only a year later these men were to put their training to the test in the slaughter of the First World War. One of the stretcher bearers in this photograph sent this postcard home, with the following words: 'RAMC, Camp Hospital, Ross. Dear Joe and Granny, Hope this finds you both quite well, this is my stretcher squad, lovely weather now best love to you both Jack'. William Blake installed the wind pump in the centre of the photograph in 1906 as part of his new water supply system for Ross. It pumped water from boreholes to a reservoir on Chase Hill.

As well as fairly serious military training for two or three weeks the Territorials' summer camps became venues for social events with sports days, concerts, cricket and football matches occupying much of the men's spare time. Evening dances were organised in the drill hall in the centre of the photograph. Soldiers' visits to local pubs were not encouraged but could not be prevented. The newspapers printed no reports of serious disturbances, and court appearances for drinking or anti-social behaviour by visiting soldiers were rare. After the horrors of the First World War – 'the war to end wars' – military training became unpopular, there were few territorial units and the camp was little used. On the outbreak of the Second World War, however, it quickly assumed a wartime role and marching soldiers were soon once again a common sight in the town. After the Second World War, with unexpected foresight, Ross UDC decided that Camp Meadow and the Golf Course should have a more practical use as an industrial estate. A variety of factories and industrial buildings now provide much needed employment for the local population.

During the stagecoach era the King's Head Hotel was the main coaching inn in Ross. Amid scenes of apparent confusion tired horses were changed for fresh ones, bags of mail were delivered to and collected from the Post Office (believed to have been situated in the hotel), passengers alighted, and luggage and parcels were unloaded. If time allowed, people could manage a quick meal before continuing their journey. After the arrival of the railway in 1855 Ross lost most of the long-distance coach traffic. Trains, however, brought visitors and, if we are to believe the advertisements, every train was met by a hotel bus. Following the railway's arrival, tourist coaching developed and extended to Ledbury, Malvern, Monmouth and Chepstow from the King's Head and the Royal Hotel. Their landlords were prepared and ready to adapt to the public's changing demands in leisure and travel.

As the use of tarmac improved road surfaces and more reliable motors made travel more predictable, people were encouraged to venture to distant attractions for a day's outing. In the relaxed post-war atmosphere of the summer of 1921, the regulars of the King's Head at Wilton Bridge went on this charabanc to see the Cheddar Gorge caves where one of the waiting local photographers took this souvenir picture. Leaning on the windscreen is Wally Nelmes, landlord of the pub. William Jenkins stands with his arm across his chest. The seated man wearing an oversized cap was Wally Burford, a farm worker. The driver, wearing a distinctive peaked cap, was Walter Baynham. From 1922 onwards the directories list Walter Baynham's daughter, Irene, as owner of what became a successful and well-remembered car hire and coach firm. Older townspeople remember how she ran this with great success from the Swan Hotel garage in Edde Cross Street for many years until the 1960s, in busy times driving the buses and taxis herself. Drivers remember her as a punctilious employer, insisting on smart dress and clean vehicles, but at the same time treating them fairly.

Even a cursory glance at this 1929 aerial photograph of Ross from the east reveals how much the town has changed in the last eighty years. Gloucester Road lies, almost traffic free, on the extreme left. At the bottom of the photograph, Victorian houses look across Smallbrook Road to the horse pasture, now built over with bungalows providing sheltered accommodation for older citizens. Ursall's monumental masons' yard next to the Secondary School can be seen in Cantilupe Road, which completes the triangle of roads in the lower part of the photograph. In the top of this triangle is the Cottage Hospital. After its demolition in 1990, retirement flats, houses and shops were built on the site. On the far side of Cantilupe Road, houses and the library now occupy the school site.

Spread over a period of about sixty years, perhaps the most significant and extensive change to the town has occurred in the area in the right of the photograph, where Llewelyn's corrugated iron garage, Broadmead and Wolverhampton Terraces in Station Street and Kemp's timber yard beyond them in Millpond Street are now only memories and photographs. School kitchens to supply children's meals were built on the site of Llewelyn's transport garage during the Second World War. After fifty years in Millpond Street Kemp's moved their timber and builders' yard to Alton Road Industrial Estate in the 1980s, when the last houses of Wolverhampton Terrace, condemned in 1934, were also demolished. First Safeways', now Morrisons', petrol station covers the Broadmead and Wolverhampton Terraces' site. Morrisons supermarket has extended its still inadequate car park over the rest of the area.

Further along Station Street, Alton Court Brewery Company owned extensive buildings on both sides of the street. Its malt house was situated in the long building in the centre of the photograph (hence the name Maltings for the modern shopping arcade nearby). It is now converted into Sainsbury's supermarket, whose car park surrounds Henry Street Evangelical church and Kemp's first timber yard.

47

This photograph from the mid 1920s shows Brook House facing the quiet junction of Greytree Road, Brampton Street and Overross Street. On the extreme right the Williams' sisters' old and dilapidated Post Office, which had become a cheap boarding house, was demolished in 1940. This provided the necessary space for a widened road junction with broad pavements and much improved visibility for the increasing traffic from the Brampton Street housing estates. On the spare ground beside the railway viaduct a public toilet and garden were built. These in turn were demolished in the 1990s to become an open air railway museum beside the red sandstone pillars of the long disused railway viaduct.

In this 1905 photograph a group of poorly clad children pose self-consciously on the pavement outside Brook House. Behind them the vacant gap in the houses in Brookend Street was later filled by George Nicholls' hardware shop. The wall on the left bordered the mill pond, which was used for centuries to drive the mill wheel, until in 1896 the owners of Town Mill installed steam power, causing the mill pond slowly to silt up. It is now a car park.

To wealthier citizens and tourists, Ross on Wye would appear to be a comfortable, handsome town, well sited on a picturesque river, but it had a poorer, shabbier side. Many houses had been cheaply built between 1750 and 1900 for the town's growing working population, who were compelled by low pay and a housing shortage to live in squalid overcrowding. The houses became dilapidated through age and neglect by private landlords who could not afford or simply refused to maintain them, and in the 1930s the Ross Urban District Council (RUDC) classed many of these houses as slums and subjected them to clearance orders. Their demolition followed as their condition was too poor for refurbishment to be economic. On this and the following four pages are illustrated some of the slums that were demolished during this period.

Wolverhampton Terrace (shown opposite and above) was a row of six poor houses facing Millpond Street. Their neat appearance from the front disguised poor quality materials and building standards, lack of privacy, bad ventilation, damp, shared toilets, inadequate water supplies and bad drainage. This photograph of the rear of the terrace reveals the one standpipe, one washhouse and one lavatory that served all the inhabitants. They were condemned by a Clearance Order in 1935. Morrisons' petrol station now stands on the site of this unsavoury terrace. Many of the inhabitants from this terrace and elsewhere in the town were rehoused in the new council estates that rose around the town between the 1920s and 1970s.

This is the rear view of No.30 Kyrle Street, owned by T.E. Bliss, just before demolition. It contained one ground floor room, its floor 2ft 8ins below ground level, and two tiny bedrooms. Like its neighbours it lacked all the amenities considered essential for decent living. There wasn't even a drainage system – the slops were simply thrown out into the street.

Nos.24, 25, 26, and 27 Overross Street have been replaced by the forecourt of Overross Garage. In the 1930s seven people lived squashed inside one of these cottages, while seven others crowded into the remaining three tiny cottages with very few facilities for washing and cooking. This view of their backyards gives some idea of the cramped and insanitary conditions the inspector found inside. With none of the facilities we now take for granted for decent living they were condemned by a Clearance Order on 24 June 1935. Griffiths extended their garage on the site.

These decrepit buildings were not peculiar to Ross. Slums like these (and often worse) could be found in some form in every village, town and city in Great Britain into the second half of the 20th century. Fortunately these blots on the townscape have been demolished, their inhabitants rehoused and their existence nearly forgotten.

Originally cheaply built at the end of the 18th century to house farm labourers, by 1930 these houses in Trenchard Street had long outlived their useful life. Signs of their decay can be seen everywhere. A brick pillar had been built to support the subsiding and crumbling corner of the upper floor of No.30. In the squalid backyard where once horses and pigs had been kept, every sort of rubbish is piled up. It must be recognised that there was such a desperate housing shortage that many people had to put up with these conditions, as unemployment or low pay restricted their choice to renting the cheapest houses available. The landlords also claimed that lack of money during the 1930s Depression hindered refurbishment.

We are fortunate that Ross Urban District Council decided they needed a photographic record of the slums before they were demolished. In 1935 they commissioned George Young, a local photographer living in Clytha House, New Street, to produce a series of photographs of the houses affected. Few such photographs of slum clearances anywhere else now exist.

A desperate national housing shortage followed the end of the Second World War, created by a million bomb-damaged houses and an acute shortage of building materials to repair them or build new replacements. With such pressure on housing, anything faintly habitable was pressed into use. After the soldiers had moved out of the Army camp in Alton Road, their huts became a German POW camp. (A few of these men later settled in Ross on Wye.) As soon as the Germans had been repatriated, desperate civilians rapidly filled the empty buildings. If some families had initially 'squatted' unofficially in the redundant Army huts, Ross UDC moved quickly to regularise the position and charged them rent, though facilities on the site were quite inadequate with poor toilet facilities and shared water taps. One unforgettable feature of the 'Camp Meadow Estate' huts was the noise the rain made on their metal roofs. Mrs Hilda Taylor and her mother-in-law May Taylor stand in the doorway watching her son George and his little sister in the summer of 1947. Gradually people were rehoused and the land was developed for industrial use. Some of the huts found alternative uses elsewhere and still survive.

An aerial view of the Vine Tree Caravan Park in the late 1960s disguises actual conditions on the ground. Such was the housing shortage in the area in 1986 that Ross UDC gave Ross and Whitchurch Rural District Council a small piece of unused land inside the cemetery entrance to temporarily site three caravans for homeless families. This land is just visible in the top left-hand corner. The very poor conditions which the tenants had to endure persuaded the Rural District Council to issue three summonses against the lessee for failing to maintain the site properly. Unable to face the consequences of his mismanagement, he absconded before the third court hearing. In the mid 1970s the brewery, who also owned the pub, sold the site for £8,000. The new owner spent a considerable sum installing mains water, a sewage system, a reliable electricity supply, a new road and hard-standings for the mobile homes, completely transforming the area. Careful scrutiny reveals that the pub's cellar door is open for a delivery of beer from the white lorry. Opposite the pub a herd of Friesian dairy cows were housed in the farm barns. Apart from the buildings bordering Walford Road, the farm was demolished in 2004/5 to make room for an estate of sixty-five new houses.

Comparing this 2005 photograph with that opposite shows the increased density of the mobile homes and how the site has been smartened in the intervening thirty years. The cemetery has started to fill after the closure of the churchyard for burials. Twenty-five allotments have been created in what was the field above the cemetery. In 2008 the number of allotment holders increased to forty-two after the absorption of the adjacent 'green strip', where a distinctive white path up the centre has been worn by young motor cyclists practising their off-road skills. Across the bottom of the photograph are some of the cheap Reema houses constructed in 1976. They stood only a few years before untreatable rust problems revealed the inadequacy of their basic design, leading inevitably to their demolition in 2008. The replacement new homes were completed in December 2009 and also covered the old car park.

At first sight this ruin appears to be the result of bomb damage or a gas explosion. It was, however, one of the council houses, built in haste in 1938 at Three Crosses, which after twenty-five years of use, were designated as sub-standard, demolished and rebuilt. Local stories blame undiscovered underground springs for causing subsidence. There are still a few of the original 1938 design houses standing.

Houses were not only demolished because of their poor construction or inadequate standards for modern living. Some just stood in the way of progress. Merrivale Lane was originally just a track to a farm but when new housing estates were built at Merrivale it had to be widened and the road junction enlarged for traffic access and safety, which necessitated the demolition of the house shown. Before the days of Health and Safety regulations a workman balances on the wall he is knocking down. In the background stands the white-painted Alton House.

Pubs had long been one of the places in Ross where people, at least initially mainly men, could find entertainment away from work and home. However the advent of the car opened up other opportunities and then the drink driving laws were introduced, contributing to many pubs' demise nationally – and locally. Forty-one pubs and hotels existed in Ross according to trade directories in 1902 and 1909, of which only fourteen are still trading (though their ranks have been joined by more recent arrivals). Although the clientele may have been predominantly male, at least eight of the pubs were run by women. Long before the Suffragettes' publicity campaign brought the subject of female franchise to the public's attention, women across the country had quietly demanded recognition and opportunities for employment. The landladies who ran the pubs in Ross, for predominantly male customers, were an important, if silent, part of this emancipation movement.

The above photograph shows the interior of the unusual Hole in the Wall pub in St Mary's Street. Originally opened as the Wine Vaults in the 1840s, Henry Morris became landlord 90 years later. After his death in 1942 his widow, Florence, decreed that nothing should be moved. Her wishes were respected, but, for some unknown reason, the pub became known locally as 'the Hole in the Wall'. Her son kept it running and as the cobwebs grew and the dust deepened in this strange memorial, it became a minor tourist attraction. In the 1970s, when the pub finally closed after Florence's death, many of the antique contents were auctioned, some finding a new home in Roger di Palma's short-lived Lost Street Museum in Brookend Street.

Dressed in their Sunday best a group of men and boys pose outside the Game Cock Inn in Brampton Street at the start of a day's outing. Richard Raynes was landlord here in 1902. The Game Cock (originally named the Old Gamecock Inn) stood on the west side of Brampton Street about thirty yards above the railway viaduct. All sign of it has vanished, even the steps from the raised pavement to the road below. In the 1950s trade deteriorated as many of its neighbours and customers in Brampton Street were moved to new houses. Mr Allen, the landlord of this cheerful pub, became a casualty of the slum clearances as his trade ebbed away. At the time most of his customers lived in the fifty houses that lined Brampton Street, of which only three survived the clearance orders. Though fondly remembered, it finally closed in 1958 and was sold to a builder who demolished it a few years later as part of a building development.

Another pub that disappeared in the last century was the Black House Inn. A 1902 directory lists Mrs Fanny Hillier as landlady of the Travellers Rest Black House. As part of the tide of progress, soon after the M50 was completed the old buildings were swept away, to be replaced by the present Travellers' Rest, which perpetuates the old name. The original buildings stood on the junction of the Ledbury and Newent roads, somewhere underneath the car park of the popular new pub.

Another form of entertainment was provided by the various celebrations of events of national importance, and by local carnivals and parades. An eye-witness account was given of the festivities in Ross marking King George V and Queen Mary's Coronation on 6 June 1911 on this postcard showing part of the procession in Gloucester Road: 'My Dear Father, The festivities here were great & surpassed expectations in the decorations and illuminations part of it. I joined in the grand procession to the Church in the morning as a member of the Druids. You can see part of the procession on this pc so you can gather by it that it fell little short of the grand affair in London. The weather was stormy in the morning & evening but in the afternoon it favoured a cricket match which I took part in against the S. Wales Borderers, which ended in a draw. The Coronation brought me no luck in the scoring line, as I was run out for no runs. In the evening there was an open air concert in the Prospect. Saturday the cricket match was against Ledbury, we got well beaten. I made 11 runs & was then caught at the wicket. Starting evening work at the Bank now. Yr affectionate son Bertie.'

Union Flags decorate Gloucester Road for the 1919 Peace procession.

Employees of G. Hall's Ross Tyre Rerubbering Co., from the Royal Hotel Garage, decorated their van as a swan for their entry in the 1926 Carnival parade. The usual large crowds of appreciative townspeople and visitors lined the roads three or four deep to watch the imaginative and colourful procession pass by in bright summer sunshine.

Various explanations have been suggested for the strange name Larruperz, which was assumed by a group of spirited young Ross musicians who amused themselves by forming a dance orchestra in 1921 and playing the lively ragtime music then in fashion. Soon realising their musical talents could make money, they started serious fundraising to help the community of Ross. In 1932 they helped fund a much needed ambulance for the St John Ambulance Association. Ambitious ideas for a new modern public hall took root and grew. Seizing their chance in 1936, they purchased a slum clearance site in Edde Cross Street, overlooking the Wye, for £265. Members spent a reported 544 hours of their own time clearing the site of the rubble of its derelict houses. Their plans were thwarted by the Second World War, when the site became a 'temporary' car park; part of it is still a car park to this day. A fifty year delay followed, until their plans finally bore fruit in 1989, when protracted negotiations over a property deal resulted in a massive windfall of £320,000. The Ross on Wye and District Community Association, (the organisation to which the Larruperz had transferred its assets), was able to utilise this huge windfall to help fund the conversion of the redundant Grammar School building into the Larruperz Centre. At long last its opening on 22 June 1990 realised the cherished sixty year old dreams of the 'Pioneer' group of young Ross musicians. Its continued success in a variety of activities has silenced the critics who said it wouldn't survive! Many feel that the ambitions and achievements of this group of public-spirited young Ross men should never be forgotten. On 6 July 1927 R.E. Davies photographed five of the members of the Larruperz Wye Valley Orchestra as they prepared to play music for the Ross Hospital Carnival procession and for the dance later that evening. The band included Ivan V. Constance (trumpet), N.F. Tristram-Blay (saxophone), A.E.R. Paton (violin), R.W. Bushnell (piano), E.J. Kearsey (drums), C.S. Constance (violin & banjo) and sometimes others.

Standing outside the Kyrle Picture Palace, friends of the Wye Valley orchestra, otherwise known as the Larruperz, prepare their float for a 1920s carnival procession. Their placards advertise that evening's Carnival Dance at the Railway Hotel.

Traffic-free Smallbrook Road was a convenient assembly point for processions. On the right ponies graze by the brook in the meadow now covered with old people's sheltered retirement bungalows. The building in the distance is the Phoenix coal office, which was demolished in 2011.

Apparently photographed
from an upstairs window
of the Kyrle Picture Palace,
this appears to be the
tail end of a procession
entering Gloucester Road
from Cantilupe Road. The
row of shops including
the one now occupied by
the gift shop Crows Feet
was built in 1922 on the
triangle of empty land
between Henry Street and
Cantilupe Road just visible
in the top centre.

Another very popular form of entertainment was the cinema, as indicated by the presence of the Kyrle Picture Palace in the backdrop to the previous photograph. At the age of 50, Edwin Dekins became a household name in Ross when he built its first permanent cinema – the Kyrle Picture Palace – which provided entertainment for generations of townspeople for the next forty years. Edwin (Ted) Dekins had been born in 1863 into a large family in Brookend Street. His father was a building contractor. With an eye open for any self-employment opportunity his home town offered, Edwin started his career as a hairdresser and tobacconist in the High Street in 1892. His antique business started almost by accident when someone offered to buy a pair of chairs he had renovated and placed on the pavement for want of room in the shop. Seeing the potential in old furniture he quickly bought more and his antique business took off. Ever ambitious and seeing the chance to make some money in the first years of the century, he pioneered cinematographic shows in the town and villages around. The first purpose-built cinema in the country was opened in 1908. Five years later, in 1913, Dekins realised the cinema's popular appeal and commissioned William Bevan to build the Kyrle Picture Palace to plans by the firm of Small and Ashton. This was in Gloucester Road opposite the Cantilupe Road junction. The cinema's auditorium seated 200, with another 50 seats in the balcony. Backstage were changing rooms for the variety acts who he engaged to entertain the audience in the intervals between films. Styling himself 'Professor Dekins', he wrote a booklet called *Hints on Conjuring*. He loved entertaining children with his conjuring and sleight of hand and would sometimes put on a conjuring act to entertain the audience if an act failed to arrive. If possible he changed his film shows twice a week, advertising them and the supporting acts extensively. The Kyrle Picture Palace's popularity is well demonstrated by this crowd of both poor and well-dressed children which fills Gloucester Road before entrance to a children's Saturday film show sometime in the 1920s. In the 1950s the price of a ticket for children's Saturday morning entertainment was 6d (2½p). Today's constant traffic along this road would render such a gathering and photograph impossible. In the 1920s Dekins' antique shop, run by his sister Dolly, was beside the cinema.

Records show that the educational needs of Ross's children have been reasonably well served by schools of various types for at least the last three hundred years and maybe longer. There were smart boarding schools for the children of the gentry who could afford the fees, and free schools for the less fortunate. For most there were packed schoolrooms and 'dame schools' where a penny bought a week's basic education in the three 'Rs' (reading, writing and arithmetic).

Until 1891 there was nothing standard about schooling in Britain. Education was not high on the agenda of Victorian Britain, teachers were not trained or qualified, and anyone could open a school if they could find enough pupils. Churches ran schools of varying standards, focussing mainly on learning the Scriptures. Alongside were the 'Ragged Schools', run for poor children with accordingly low standards. Many of the wealthy worried that educated people would not tolerate the shocking conditions then prevalent in industry, agriculture and service. Farmers considered it quite unnecessary for their workers to be able to read and write, whilst poor families were suspicious of education because it often cost money they could not afford and kept children in school when they could have been earning money at work. Although the employment of children aged under ten was forbidden under an Act of 1833, there were not enough inspectors to enforce it.

The 1870 School Act divided the country into districts, each with an education board. These board schools attracted better teachers thanks to enhanced wages. In 1880 school attendance became compulsory for children between five and ten and in 1891 education was made free of charge. In 1899 the school leaving age was raised to 12, soon to be raised to 14 by the 1903 Employment of Children Act, in an effort to improve the levels of reading, writing, arithmetic and general knowledge among the workforce. The 1947 Education Act led to the education system we broadly know today.

Ross Secondary School facing Ryefield Road soon after its opening in 1912. Two years later its name was changed to Ross Grammar School to attract more government funding.

High School, Ross.

Squeezed between the former rectory garden wall and Copse Cross Street, Claireville House has had a varied history, and is now a private house partially screened from traffic by trees. In the 1860s Madame du Beau and Miss Wolstenholme founded a girls' boarding school here, which in 1909 was run by Miss Annie Palmer and Miss Laura Hancock B.A. The photograph shows the school in 1907, someone having added the words 'High School, Ross'.

Opposite: An aerial view from the west of Ross on Wye Secondary Modern School at Overross soon after its opening at the beginning of the summer term in April 1953. Mr W. Jeans, the headmaster, presided over 23 staff and 500 children from Ross and the surrounding villages in what was then the most modern school in Herefordshire. The school had taken three years to build and almost a million bricks were used in its structure. It is now difficult to conceive that, reflecting the thinking of the time, the school was initially designed solely for boys. A separate school for girls was to be built at a later date – an idea quietly forgotten as ideas changed. A swimming pool was added in June 1960 after it was discovered that only 25 pupils could swim, and extra classrooms for cookery and geography were also added as numbers rose, boosted by the attendance of girls. By the autumn of 1979 the number of children had grown to 800, who were then joined by the 400 pupils from Ross Grammar School to form the Comprehensive John Kyrle High School. Note how many houses now fill the gaps along Ledbury Road that runs diagonally across the top of the photograph, which also shows the children apparently filing onto the sports field to watch a football match.

After the Second World War, as road traffic grew in both volume and size, problems with the nation's road infrastructure became increasingly apparent. This photograph looks along the High Street from the Market Hall towards what is now Lloyds TSB bank. By 1950 it was obvious that the High Street, along which the A40 was routed, was more suitable for the horse-drawn traffic it was built for than the massive loads forced to use it. Heavy loads were tolerated during the Second World War, but the centuries-old street could never accommodate the heavy traffic driving through the town after the war. Eventually this pressure led to the widening and strengthening of Wilton Bridge and the building of by-passes round the town that have yet to be completed to the south. Wynne's of Newport owned these two massive Thorneycroft tractor units propelling a 99-feet long load through the town centre. As it inched its way along the High Street towards Wilton, people came out of the shops to watch. At this date all Ross on Wye's streets were two way, so that the police could divert cars and lorries round the town until a heavy load like this had safely passed the narrow High Street bottleneck. As part of its campaign for better roads, the *Ross Gazette* often reported similar scenes until the M50 and the A40 by-pass were finally completed in 1960.

After the end of the Second World War many, including the Council for the Preservation of Rural England, campaigned for the restoration of Wilton Bridge to its former width of 18 feet, without suggesting any solution to the town's traffic problems. This was the position when the M50 and the A40 dual carriageway to south Wales were opened in 1960, with traffic from Gloucester and the Forest of Dean still forced to go through the town to join the new roads at Overross or Wilton. This photograph shows Richard Read, owner of the haulage company advertised on the lorry, directing operations to raise the town's 1969 Christmas lights above his lorry's oversized load, as it tries to negotiate the narrow High Street. In the background a policeman can be seen redirecting traffic down Broad Street. In 1985 the eastern relief road opened, eliminating some of the town centre congestion.

In March 1958 up to 300 men began building what was the second motorway in Britain – the M50, often called the Ross Spur. When it opened in November 1960, however, it was a road to nowhere, as the M5 from Birmingham to Strensham was not completed until late 1962! Its continuation, the A40 by-pass, was constructed with a purpose-built lay-by inspection area at Overross where police could carry out traffic checks. Photographed soon after its opening in 1960, seven policemen busily inspect cars and lorries for defects, overloading and incorrect paperwork.

In 1985 work proceeds on surfacing the new slip road to the east-bound services as part of the ancillary work for a new roundabout and relief road on the eastern side of Ross on Wye. Twenty years later these services were demolished, and the slip road now leads into Labels car park. The houses of Oak Rise have been built on the land in the middle distance and on the extreme right the Brampton Abbotts road bridge is just visible.

Another traffic problem. The calm of a winter afternoon in Gloucester Road was shattered when this van from London crashed into the doorway of the Cheltenham and Gloucester Building Society. A policeman was soon on the scene to hear the driver's explanation while an interested lady shopper watched intently.

On hand if needed, and on duty at public events, was the Ross St John's Ambulance Brigade, formed *circa* 1909 as a result of the determination of G. Kemp. In 1934, with financial assistance from many organisations in the town, the Brigade raised enough funds to purchase this Austin 20 ambulance. It was kept at Passey & Sons' garage in Gloucester Road and regularly attended accidents and transported people to hospital. Three years later, in 1937, the Brigade bought three adjoining slum clearance sites in Edde Cross Street, where, after another year spent raising the necessary £1,000, they built a permanent headquarters and garage. Its crew of three pose for this wartime photograph. To conform to wartime blackout regulations, the ambulance had had its mudguards, the edge of the running boards and roof painted white for improved night-time visibility. Slitted hoods covered the large headlights to minimise glare that could be visible to enemy aircraft. On the left of the doorway a wall of sandbags had been erected as protection from enemy bomb blast.

Another source of emergency help, though hopefully infrequently needed, was the fire service. In 1899, during Frederick Cooper's energetic chairmanship, the Fire Brigade Committee raised £418 4s 6d to purchase a new Shand Mason fire engine for the combined Ross Urban and Ross Rural District Councils. The appliance cost £325 with an additional £83 8s 10d for an escape ladder, uniforms for the men, axes, belts, helmets, miscellaneous equipment and a cheque book! The cost of raising this subscription was £9 15s 8d for correspondence, postage stamps and small sundry amounts, which were all meticulously detailed in Cooper's account book. This 1910 photograph by R.E. Davies shows some of the fire crew with Alfred

Bird, the fire brigade captain, posing with a trophy beside their appliances at their garage in St Mary's Street. It is a sobering thought that these days we take the work of the rescue services for granted, but in the 19th century the fire brigade presented a bill for every incident it attended. In 1879 the Ross Fire Brigade Committee laid down the following list of charges: within four miles of the town the charge was £4 4s and for every mile beyond that 10s 6d. For every fireman attending a fire in the town the charge was 4s 6d, and in the country areas 7s 6d – from which the men received one shilling (5p) per hour. Despite this considerable investment in time and money, the Fire Brigade was dependent on horses from the Royal Hotel's stables and 'call out' times were slow. The situation deteriorated so much during the First World War, when most of the suitable horses had been requisitioned by the Army, that farmers were requested to send their own horses to pull the fire engine to a fire on their property!

During the Second World War George Barnett was leading fireman in Ross on Wye, and he is seen here delivering a message to a Women's Voluntary Service clerk in the control room. The role the WVS played in the Second World War is often forgotten, and in Ross, as in many other places, they staffed the control room, thus releasing men for other duties. The wall boards in the background show the telephone numbers of fire stations from Cardiff and Bristol, as well as Worcestershire and Herefordshire, and the telephone numbers of other local services in case of need. Note the old-style telephone and the ledgers with records written in pen and ink, all of which would now be computerised.

This Dennis fire engine was in service in Ross on Wye from 1969, but only its bell remains in the town for the engine itself ended its days in Rhyl. The driver is Tony Bridges, and standing alongside are Station Officer Reg Meekes, fireman Reg Lillewall and leading fireman Aubrey Lerego, who was well known to many people in the town for his musical talents. In 1968 Ross on Wye's small fire station moved from its cramped position between the churchyard and the Royal Hotel, now the site of the Phoenix Theatre, to its present modern building at Hildersley.

One of the firemen involved in fighting some dramatic fires kept photographs as mementoes. Here, spectacular flames leap up to roof height from the Seven Seas fish and chip shop in Broad Street as firemen start work to extinguish the blaze. (The date of this fire is unknown.)

Bales of hay and straw blaze out of control as Ross on Wye's firemen start to tackle a farm fire, believed to be at Walford.

Index